A STEP INTO HISTORY™

WORLD WAR I

BY STEVEN OTFINOSKI

Series Editor
Elliott Rebhun, Editor & Publisher,
The New York Times Upfront
at Scholastic

SCHOLASTIC

Content Consultant: James Marten, PhD, Professor and Chair, History
Department, Marquette University, Milwaukee, Wisconsin

Cover: A machine gunner during World War I

Library of Congress Cataloging-in-Publication Data
Names: Otfinoski, Steven, author.Title: World War I / by Steven Otfinoski.
Description: New York : Children's Press, [2017] | Series: A Step into history |
Includes bibliographical references and index. Identifiers: LCCN 2016025138|
ISBN 9780531225714 (library binding) | ISBN 9780531243657 (pbk.)
Subjects: LCSH: World War, 1914–1918—Juvenile literature. Classification:
LCC D522.7 .O75 2017 | DDC 940.3—dc23
LC record available at https://lccn.loc.gov/2016025138

1 2 3 4 5 6 7 8 9 10 R 26 25 24 23 22 21 20 19 18 17

CONTENTS

PROLOGUE 6

THE TWO SIDES IN WORLD WAR I 10

MAPS 12

CHAPTER 1 • A RECIPE FOR WAR 14

CHAPTER 2 • GERMANY'S LAST EMPEROR 18

CHAPTER 3 • DEATH OF AN ARCHDUKE 22

CHAPTER 4 • THE SIDES LINE UP 26

CHAPTER 5 • AMERICA STAYS NEUTRAL 30

CHAPTER 6 • MIRACLE AT THE MARNE 34

CHAPTER 7 • DOWN IN THE TRENCHES 38

CHAPTER 8 • POETS AT WAR 42

CHAPTER 9 • THE CHRISTMAS TRUCE 46

CHAPTER 10 • TRAGEDY AT GALLIPOLI 50

CHAPTER 11 • DANGER BENEATH THE SEA 54

CHAPTER 12 • **A DEADLY NEW WEAPON** **58**

CHAPTER 13 • **A CLASH AT SEA** **62**

CHAPTER 14 • **KNIGHTS OF THE AIR** **66**

CHAPTER 15 • **THE BLOODIEST BATTLE OF THE WAR** **70**

CHAPTER 16 • **TANKS ON THE BATTLEFIELD** **74**

CHAPTER 17 • **MATA HARI—SPY** **78**

CHAPTER 18 • **THE RUSSIAN REVOLUTION** **82**

CHAPTER 19 • **AMERICA GOES TO WAR** **86**

CHAPTER 20 • **WOMEN IN WAR** **90**

CHAPTER 21 • **SERGEANT YORK, AMERICAN HERO** **94**

CHAPTER 22 • **PROPAGANDA: THE WAR OF
WORDS AND IMAGES** **98**

CHAPTER 23 • **AFRICAN AMERICAN SOLDIERS** **102**

CHAPTER 24 • **SONGS OF WAR** **106**

CHAPTER 25 • **THE WAR REACHES A CROSSROADS** **110**

CHAPTER 26 • **THE WAR'S END** **114**

CHAPTER 27 • **THE TREATY OF VERSAILLES** **118**

CHAPTER 28 • **THE GREAT PANDEMIC** **122**

CHAPTER 29 • **THE LEAGUE OF NATIONS** **126**

CHAPTER 30 • **A WORLD IN TATTERS** **130**

KEY PLAYERS **134**
WORLD WAR I TIMELINE **136**
GLOSSARY **140**
FIND OUT MORE **142**
INDEX **143**
ABOUT THE AUTHOR **144**

PROLOGUE

THE LATE 19TH CENTURY AND EARLY 20TH century was a time of relative peace for Europe. Science and technology had improved the lives of millions. Homes had running water and electricity for the first time. New industries created jobs for people, giving them higher wages and more money to spend. Inventions like the automobile and movies meant that families could enjoy their leisure time in new ways. European countries such as France, England, and Germany were now industrial giants. They each had empires that encompassed three continents.

But beneath the wealth and prosperity, there were powerful tensions between these nations. At the beginning of the 20th century, countries took sides against each other in old and new **alliances.** And in the summer of 1914, this led to a war unlike any previous conflict in history. The same technology that had improved life was now being used to kill people in new and horrible ways. An entire generation of young men were killed or wounded as the war quickly engulfed much of the world. The United States, an ocean away, would be

You will find the definitions of bold words in the glossary on pages 140-41.

drawn into the war three years later and help to win it.

Today, this global conflict is known as World War I, but at the time people called it the Great War. When it ended in November 1919, nobody thought that an even greater war would soon follow: World War II.

Soldiers used bugle calls to keep in touch with distant troops during World War I.

THE TWO SIDES IN WORLD WAR I

THE ALLIES

Dates in parentheses show when each country entered the war.

SERBIA
(July 28, 1914)

RUSSIA
(August 1, 1914)

FRANCE
(August 3, 1914)

BELGIUM
(August 4, 1914)

GREAT BRITAIN AND ITS COLONIES AND COMMONWEALTH NATIONS
(August 4, 1914)

ITALY
(May 23, 1915)

PORTUGAL
(March 9, 1916)

ROMANIA
(August 27, 1916)

UNITED STATES
(April 6, 1917)

GREECE
(June 27, 1917)

THE CENTRAL POWERS

AUSTRIA-HUNGARY
(July 28, 1914)

GERMANY
(August 1, 1914)

OTTOMAN (TURKISH) EMPIRE
(October 29, 1914)

BULGARIA
(October 14, 1915)

MAPS

THE TWO SIDES IN WORLD WAR I

The Central powers were led by Germany and Austria-Hungary. The Allies were led by Great Britain and France and, later, the United States.

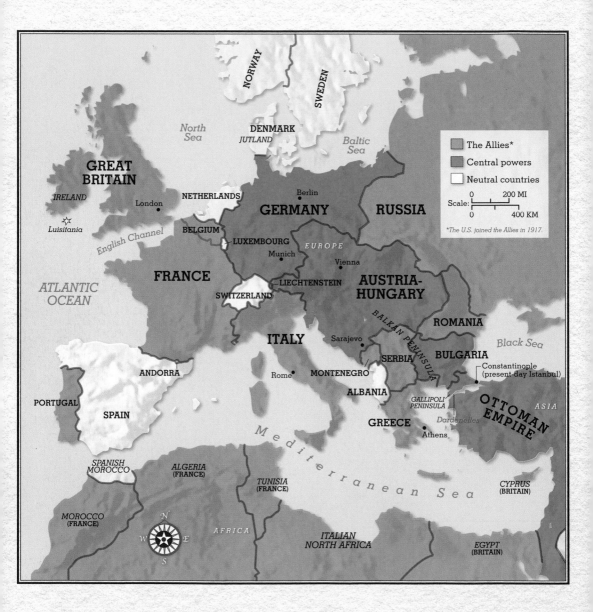

THE WESTERN FRONT AT THE BEGINNING OF WORLD WAR I (1914)

Many of the war's biggest battles took place to the west of Germany, near the 400-mile (644-kilometer) Western front.

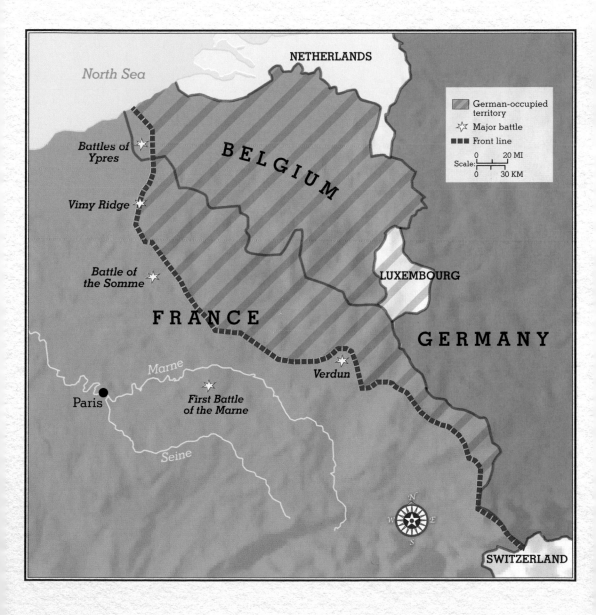

NETHERLANDS

North Sea

German-occupied territory

Major battle

Front line

Scale: 0   20 MI
        0   30 KM

BELGIUM

Battles of Ypres

Vimy Ridge

LUXEMBOURG

Battle of the Somme

FRANCE

GERMANY

Marne

Verdun

Paris

First Battle of the Marne

Seine

SWITZERLAND

During World War I, soldiers wore hard helmets like this one to protect their heads during combat.

CHAPTER 1

A RECIPE FOR WAR

Wars don't happen overnight. There is often a long period of unrest and tension that precedes them. World War I was no exception.

I N THE LATE 1800s, GERMANY AND FRANCE HAD been bitter enemies. Germany had the more powerful military. It had defeated France in the Franco-Prussian War of 1870–71 and was prepared to fight again.

To help protect against potential attack from Germany, French leaders sought alliances with other European countries. Both Great Britain and Russia pledged that they would come to France's aid if an enemy attacked.

Germany made similar alliances with Austria-Hungary and Italy. Germany's leaders were planning an attempt to take control of all of Europe. They were simply waiting for an excuse to go to war with France and its allies.

Prussian (German) forces occupy France during the Franco-Prussian War.

A German artillery observation unit

CHAPTER 2

GERMANY'S LAST EMPEROR

The man most responsible for sparking
the events leading to World War I was
Kaiser (Emperor) Wilhelm II.

Find out more about people whose names appear in orange and bold on pages 134-35.

BORN WITH A PARALYZED LEFT ARM, **Kaiser (Emperor) Wilhelm II** set out to prove his manhood when he took the throne in 1888. He was an arrogant, impulsive man with great national ambitions for Germany. The German people liked and supported these ambitions.

Wilhelm, with the encouragement of Germany's military leaders, wanted a colonial empire that would equal that of Germany's rival, Great Britain. To fulfill his plans, he built a large navy. He boasted that Germany, not Great Britain, would soon rule the sea.

The kaiser was no diplomat, and he made enemies easily. His attempts to exert influence in French-held Morocco in North Africa almost led to war with France. His blunders drew France and Great Britain closer together against him.

Kaiser Wilhelm II takes a morning ride on his horse in 1910.

Archduke Franz Ferdinand and his wife, Sophie, walk toward their car in Sarajevo minutes before their assasination

CHAPTER 3

DEATH OF AN ARCHDUKE

One man's murder was the spark that
finally ignited World War I.

O N THE MORNING OF SUNDAY, JUNE 28, 1914, Archduke Franz Ferdinand of Austria-Hungary (now the separate nations of Austria and Hungary) and his wife, Sophie, were in Sarajevo, the capital of Bosnia, a **province** of Austria. As they traveled to Sarajevo's city hall for a reception, a man threw a bomb at their car. The bomb bounced off the car before exploding and injuring several bystanders. Ferdinand and Sophie arrived safely at city hall.

Archduke Franz Ferdinand: was the heir to the Austrian throne.

After the reception, they traveled back along the same route they had taken earlier that day. This time they were not so lucky. Nineteen-year-old Gavrilo Princip fired two shots at the royal couple as their car stopped alongside him. Sophie died almost instantly. The archduke died on the way to the hospital.

Princip and the man who threw the bomb that morning had been working together to kill Franz Ferdinand. As Serbians, they were angry at the way the government of Austria-Hungary treated Serbs and other minorities. Princip was arrested and died in prison in 1918. By that time, more than 15 million people had died in the war that had resulted from his actions.

The bodies of Franz Ferdinand and his wife lie in state at the Imperial Palace in Vienna, Austria.

British troops pass through the coastal town of Ostend, Belgium, in August 1914.

CHAPTER 4

THE SIDES LINE UP

After the Archduke's assassination,
a quarrel between two countries
quickly engulfed many more.

THE PEOPLE OF AUSTRIA-HUNGARY WERE shocked by the archduke's death and blamed Serbia. Things quickly spun out of control:

- Encouraged by its German allies, Austria-Hungary declared war on Serbia on July 28, 1914.
- In response, **Czar (Emperor) Nicholas II** of Russia began mobilizing the huge Russian army to defend Serbia.
- France, which had pledged to support Russia, also prepared for war.
- Germany responded by declaring war on Russia on August 1 and France on August 3.

  Between Germany and France lay the small country of Belgium.

- Germany invaded Belgium in an effort to reach France.
- Great Britain, another French ally, entered the war on France's side (the Allies).
- In October 1914, the Ottoman (Turkish) Empire entered the war on the side of Germany and Austria-Hungary (the Central powers).
- In May 1915, Italy joined the Allies.

Czar Nicholas II of Russia (right) meets with President Raymond Poincare of France (left) in 1914.

THE ALLIES
SERBIA

RUSSIA

FRANCE

BELGIUM

GREAT BRITAIN

ITALY

THE CENTRAL POWERS
AUSTRIA-HUNGARY

GERMANY

OTTOMAN (TURKISH) EMPIRE

The complete list of countries on each side of the war, as well as the dates they entered the war, can be found on pages 10–11.

Many Americans spoke out loudly that they did not want their country to enter the war.

CHAPTER 5

AMERICA STAYS NEUTRAL

The nations of Europe had taken sides, but no one knew where the United States would stand.

AS WAR ERUPTED IN EUROPE, MOST Americans agreed with **President Woodrow Wilson** that the United States should stay "**neutral** in fact as well as in name." But while they didn't necessarily want to participate in combat, many Americans favored either the Allies or the Central powers, often depending on their country of origin. Others simply did not care what happened somewhere as far away as Europe.

No matter what they felt about the war, most Americans believed it would quickly end in a peace treaty without a clear winner. As for President Wilson, he cared little for foreign affairs and was more interested in domestic issues. When he ran for re-election in 1916, his campaign slogan proudly boasted that he was the man who "kept [the United States] out of war."

President Woodrow Wilson marches in a parade to celebrate the first Flag Day in Washington, D.C., on June 14, 1916.

President Wilson created Flag Day, a holiday that is still celebrated today.

CHAPTER 6

MIRACLE AT THE MARNE

The Germans believed they would crush
France easily. Despite their confidence,
the Germans were in for a surprise.

THE GERMAN ARMY HAD THE BEST TRAINING and equipment in Europe. Its soldiers used cutting-edge weapons such as machine guns that could fire up to 600 rounds a minute. They also used powerful **artillery** weapons. The Germans wore gray uniforms that provided good camouflage from enemy guns.

French soldiers, on the other hand, continued to wear their traditional red trousers and bright blue jackets. The German army also used more effective tactics that limited the number of soldiers lost. It seemed like Germany would quickly win the war.

Then came the Battle of the Marne in northern France in September 1914. At one point during the eight-day battle, French forces were so desperate that reinforcements were sped to the **front** in taxicabs. German scouts could see the spire of the Eiffel Tower in Paris, just 14 miles (22.5 kilometers) away. But they came no closer to the French capital. Incredibly, their superior army was beaten back by the stubborn French forces. They were forced to retreat. German hopes of a swift victory were dashed. It was going to be a long, hard-fought war.

French soldiers climb over a barricade during the Battle of the Marne in 1914.

Soldiers often carried shovels to help dig trenches.

CHAPTER 7

DOWN IN THE TRENCHES

World War I introduced a new style of combat that saw soldiers spending most of their time in ditches.

THERE WERE TWO MAIN FRONTS IN THE war. The eastern front was to the east of Germany, and the western front to the west. As 1914 drew to a close, the fighting on the Western Front had reached a stalemate, with neither side able to dislodge the other. Soldiers fought from trenches dug out of the ground. They stretched about 400 miles (644 km) across the continent from Belgium to Switzerland. The trenches had to be deep enough so a soldier could stand in them without exposing his head as a target. A raised platform in a trench allowed soldiers to shoot over the top during an attack.

In places, enemy trenches were separated by only 100 to 200 yards (91 to 183 meters). The space between was known, for good reason, as no-man's-land. Some German trenches were well made, with concrete **bunkers** for living and sleeping. French trenches were not built as well. They were mere dirt and were infested by rats and lice that made the soldiers sick. Heavy rains left soldiers standing in water for days. This led to the dreaded disease called trench foot. Feet became so diseased that in some cases they had to be amputated. Despite the conditions, both sides fought with courage . . . and cruelty.

German soldiers in a trench in 1915

These German soldiers are drinking french wine!

66 *If I should die, think only this of me,*
That there's some corner of a foreign field
That is forever England. 99

—RUPERT BROOKE

CHAPTER 8

POETS AT WAR

Some soldiers expressed their feelings about
the conflict through their writing, displaying
very different attitudes toward war.

THE YOUNG MEN WHO WENT OFF TO WAR in 1914 saw themselves as gallant heroes fighting for a good cause. Among them was the English poet Rupert Brooke. His war poems are filled with patriotism and idealism. Brooke died not in combat, but from an infection he suffered while serving on an island in the Aegean Sea in 1915.

Another English poet-soldier, Wilfred Owen, saw the war very differently. He served in the trenches in France and suffered a mental breakdown. While in a hospital, Owen began to write poems that depicted the horrors of war. His feelings are summed up in the title of one of his most famous poems, "Anthem for Doomed Youth." Owen yearned for peace but didn't live to see it. He was killed in action one week before the war ended.

The United States had its soldier poets, too. Perhaps the most famous was Alan Seeger, who volunteered to fight for France. He died in action on July 4, 1916. His poem "I Have a Rendezvous with Death" was a favorite of future U.S. president John F. Kennedy.

German soldiers use their downtime to write letters and document their time in the trenches.

DECEMBER 24

The Christmas Truce

AUG **SEP** **OCT** NOV DEC **1915** JAN FEB

CHAPTER 9

THE CHRISTMAS TRUCE

Peace in the midst of war became

a reality one Christmas Eve.

CHRISTMAS WAS A HOLIDAY OF HOPE AND love throughout Europe, even during the war. In December 1914, some 100,000 British and German troops along the western front decided to lay down their arms and celebrate the holiday in peace. The "Christmas Truce" was unofficial and spontaneous. It began on Christmas Eve as men in the trenches on both sides sang Christmas carols to each other. Some Germans even had the accompaniment of a brass band.

Unarmed Germans first ventured into no-man's-land at dawn on Christmas Day and approached British soldiers with cries of "Merry Christmas." The British soldiers left their trenches to meet them, shaking hands and exchanging small gifts such as cakes, plum puddings, and cigarettes. Some spent the day burying their dead. Others played a game of soccer. The next day, fighting resumed. Unfortunately, the Christmas Truce of 1914 was not repeated. Officers warned soldiers that if they attempted it again, they would be punished. For the remainder of the conflict, Christmas was just another day of war.

German soldiers on the eastern front gather around a Christmas tree to sing carols.

AUSTRIA-HUNGARY

EUROPE

ROMANIA

BALKAN PENINSULA

MONTENEGRO

BULGARIA

Black Sea

SERBIA

Constantinople
(present-day
Istanbul)

ALBANIA

GALLIPOLI
PENINSULA

OTTOMAN
EMPIRE

*Aegean
Sea* *Dardanelles*

ASIA

GREECE

N
W E
S

40 MILES
(64 kilometers)

CHAPTER 10

TRAGEDY AT GALLIPOLI

Few people outside of Turkey had ever
heard of Gallipoli or could find it on a map.
That would change in the spring of 1915.

THE ALLIES SAW THE 600-YEAR-OLD OTTOMAN Empire as the weakest of the Central powers and went to work to defeat it. The Ottoman Turks had shut an important shipping route between the Aegean Sea and the Black Sea to prevent Allied ships from delivering supplies to Russia.

Check out the map on page 50!

To reopen the route, French and British forces planned to attack the Turks with warships. But mines planted by the Turks blew up some of the ships and the plan had to be abandoned.

A second attempt was made in the spring of 1915. Hundreds of thousands of troops from Great Britain and ANZAC (Australian and New Zealand Army Corps) landed on Turkey's Gallipoli **Peninsula**. They wanted to drive back the Turks so the mines could be removed. The campaign was a total failure. More than 250,000 Allied soldiers were injured or killed in the attack. The 41-year-old British first lord of the Admiralty was blamed for Gallipoli and lost his job. His name was **Winston Churchill**, and he would redeem himself as Great Britain's prime minister during World War II.

British soldiers chased out of Gallipoli head for safety in Greece.

A German U-boat

CHAPTER 11

DANGER BENEATH THE SEA

Germany brought a new and dangerous
weapon into the war: U-boats.

"U-boat" is an abbreviation of *Unterseeboot*, German for "undersea boat."

WORLD WAR I WAS THE FIRST TIME submarines were used as effective weapons of war. German war submarines called <u>U-boats</u> prowled beneath the seas, inflicting heavy losses on the Allied nations' merchant ships. The U-boats were effective but a far cry from today's submarines. They could only stay underwater for several hours at a time and carried just a few torpedoes to fire at enemy ships. U-boats were also quite small. Thirty to 40 crew members lived uncomfortably in each boat's cramped quarters. However, the U-boats had a deadly power.

On May 7, 1915, a tragedy horrified the world. That day, a German U-boat sank the British passenger liner *Lusitania* off the coast of Ireland. A <u>nonmilitary ship</u>, the *Lusitania* had left New York for England six days earlier. Among the 1,198 passengers killed were 128 Americans. Great Britain accused the Germans of mass murder. President Woodrow Wilson sent strong notes of protest to the German government. The Germans agreed not to sink passenger ships again without warning, and the United States remained neutral.

German officials argued that the *Lusitania* had been carrying arms and ammunition to Europe, which was later proven to be true.

The Lusitania *sets off from New York City on May 1, 1915, to begin its final voyage.*

It took just 18 minutes for the *Lusitania* to sink.

Mortar shells like this one were used to launch poison gas at enemies.

CHAPTER 12

A DEADLY NEW WEAPON

Another, even more terrible weapon
entered the war in 1915: poison gas.

ON APRIL 22, 1915, AT THE SECOND BATTLE of Ypres in Belgium, clouds of yellowish-green fog drifted toward the French and British lines. It was deadly chlorine gas that had been released by the Germans. Hundreds of soldiers were overcome by the gas and died. Within days, Allied soldiers were equipped with gas masks to protect their lungs and eyes from the deadly chemical. Soon France developed its own poison gas, phosgene.

While somewhat effective in killing or driving back enemies, gas had one serious problem: if the wind was not blowing toward the enemy, the gas would be blown back toward its users. This problem became less of a concern when the two sides began firing gas from artillery shells.

In 1917, the Germans came up with an even deadlier concoction—mustard gas. It caused the victims' skin to blister and could also inflict blindness. It lingered on the battlefield for weeks after it was used, making the area uninhabitable. By the end of the war, 124,000 tons of chemicals had been released during combat.

German soldiers and their dogs wear gas masks to protect against chemical gas attacks.

CHAPTER 13

A CLASH AT SEA

The Battle of Jutland was the greatest
sea battle of World War I.

ON MAY 31, 1916, THE BRITISH AND GERMAN navies clashed in a battle near Jutland, off the coast of Denmark. A total of 252 warships, including 64 battleships and battle cruisers, took part in one of the greatest naval battles in history. The fight raged through the night and into the following morning.

The results were indecisive. Both sides claimed victory. The British fleet lost 14 ships and suffered 6,784 **casualties**. Of the 1,286 crew members aboard the battle cruiser *Queen Mary*, only 20 survived. However, the German fleet was forced to flee to its North Sea bases. It had lost 11 ships and suffered serious damage to 10 others, and 3,058 of its men were killed or injured. Germany never again challenged Great Britain's mastery of the oceans. Instead, Germany went back to its old policy of attacking any ship—military or nonmilitary— with U-boats.

German ships in combat during the Battle of Jutland

A French fighter plane

KNIGHTS OF THE AIR

If there was any glory in this brutal war, it didn't take place on land or sea, but in the air.

AIR BATTLES WERE A MAJOR PART OF World War I. Daring pilots in flimsy, single-seat aircraft fought each other in duels called <u>dogfights</u>. They shot at each other with machine guns mounted on their planes, and the losers usually plunged to an instant death. Most fighter pilots were able to rack up only a few "kills" before being killed themselves. But those rare pilots who managed to win several times were called aces or knights of the air.

These courageous men became legends in their own time, idolized in their home countries by adults and children alike. They included Eddie Rickenbacker of the United States, Billy Bishop of Canada, and, most famous of all, **Manfred von Richthofen** of Germany. Von Richthofen was known as the Red Baron because of the red plane he flew. He shot down 80 enemy planes before meeting his end in battle in April 1918. He was 25 years old.

French and German planes clash in a 1915 air battle.

This German plane has just been hit and will crash in just a few seconds.

BELGIUM

LUXEMBOURG

GERMANY

German-occupied
territory

Front line

Verdun

Marne

FRANCE

20 MILES
(32 kilometers)

N
W   E
S

CHAPTER 15

THE BLOODIEST
BATTLE OF THE WAR

War became full-scale slaughter when the Battle
of Verdun resulted in nearly a million casualties.

"THE FORCES OF FRANCE WILL BLEED TO death . . . whether we . . . reach our goal or not," German general Erich von Falkenhayn wrote to the kaiser on Christmas Day 1915. His "goal" was the historic French fortress town of Verdun on the Meuse River. For nearly two months, the Germans stockpiled weapons near Verdun. On February 21, 1916, they began their assault, bombarding Verdun for seven hours. It looked like the town would fall, but then French general Philippe Petain took charge of the fortress.

The resourceful Petain built a road to get supplies to the town and rotated weary soldiers out of the front line to keep them fresh. The Germans attacked without letting up for nearly 10 months and then retreated in the face of a French counterattack. The defense of Verdun gave hope to the French people and became a shining symbol of French resistance. But it came at a high price. About 500,000 French soldiers died or were wounded. Germany suffered nearly as many casualties. Verdun was indeed bloody, and it showed again that there would be no easy victory for either side.

The grave of a French soldier is marked by his rifle and helmet after the Battle of Verdun.

❝ *A huge grey object reared itself into view and slowly, very slowly, it crawled along. . . . It was a tank.* **❞**

—Canadian private Donald Fraser, journal
entry from September 15, 1916

CHAPTER 16

TANKS ON THE BATTLEFIELD

These new weapons were clumsy and crude,
but their power spread fear in the enemy.

URING THE FIGHTING AT VERDUN, BRITISH soldiers opened a new battle along the Somme River to the northwest of Verdun to draw German pressure away from the French. At the height of the battle, on September 15, 1916, they unleashed a new weapon—the armored tank. Forty-nine of these crude, clumsy machines lumbered toward the German trenches, tearing through barbed wire, climbing obstacles, and crushing trenches. The Germans had never seen such a devilish machine and fled in terror. However, there were too few tanks to achieve a real breakthrough.

By July 1917, British engineers had built a better tank, the Mark IV, and formed a Tank Corps. They unveiled 476 of their new tanks at the Battle of Cambrai in northern France. German soldiers scattered as tanks led the attack, followed by the British **infantry**. But by the end of the day, all the tanks were destroyed, broken down, or abandoned. Yet the armored tank would go on to revolutionize ground warfare.

A group of British soldiers ride atop a Mark IV tank.

During the war, spies used invisible ink to write secret messages.

CHAPTER 17

MATA HARI—SPY

The most infamous spy of World War I
was a dancer from a neutral country.

BOTH SIDES USED SPIES TO GAIN USEFUL information about the enemy's plans. People from neutral countries such as the Netherlands and Switzerland were often recruited because they could cross into enemy territory without arousing suspicion. Among the most famous war spies was a dancer from the Netherlands named <u>Mata Hari</u>. When her popularity as a dancer faded, she turned to spying for France but then supposedly became a double agent for Germany. While gathering information from French officers, Mata Hari was captured in Paris. Though she denied being a spy, an invisible ink kit found among her possessions was used as evidence against her. She was sentenced to die on October 15, 1917. Facing a firing squad, Mata Hari refused a blindfold and blew a kiss to the soldiers who were about to kill her.

The United States had spies, too. One of the most famous was Sylvanus Morley, an archaeologist who traveled across Mexico and Central America during the war, supposedly to study ancient ruins. In fact, he was studying the activities of German agents in the area and reporting back about them.

Mata Hari's story has been retold, often inaccurately, in a number of movies, at least three stage musicals, and even a ballet.

Mata Hari poses for a portrait in 1916.

NOVEMBER 7

*Vladimir Lenin and the
Bolshevik communists
seize power in Russia.*

JUN **JUL** AUG SEP OCT NOV DEC **1918**

CHAPTER 18

THE RUSSIAN REVOLUTION

Russia left the war to fight a new war
of its own—one that would change
the very nature of its government.

BY SEPTEMBER 1916, MORE THAN A MILLION Russian soldiers had been injured or killed in combat. The nation's people were weary of war and the injustices they suffered under the rule of Czar Nicholas II. The following March, the people overthrew the czar and set up a democratic government led by Alexander Kerensky.

But the Kerensky government was weak and no match for the **Bolshevik** communists led by Vladimir Lenin. The communists promised the Russian people a system where the rich would be removed from power, all property would be held in common, and society would be classless. Lenin and his followers overthrew Kerensky and seized power on November 7, 1917. The czar and his entire family were later executed by the Bolsheviks.

In December, Lenin took Russia out of the war and signed a peace treaty with Germany in March 1918. After a bloody Civil War with his opponents, Lenin emerged victorious in 1922 and established a new communist nation—the Soviet Union.

Vladimir Lenin delivers a speech in 1919.

Lenin is speaking in Moscow's famous Red Square.

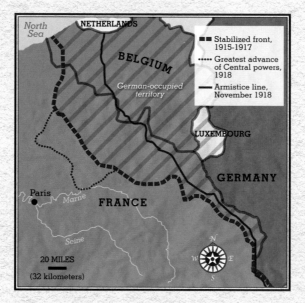

Stabilized front, 1915-1917

Greatest advance of Central powers, 1918

Armistice line, November 1918

North Sea

NETHERLANDS

BELGIUM

German-occupied territory

LUXEMBOURG

GERMANY

Paris

Marne

FRANCE

Seine

20 MILES

(32 kilometers)

N
W   E
S

CHAPTER 19

AMERICA GOES TO WAR

Renewed German aggression changed
American attitudes about joining the war.

ON JANUARY 31, 1917, GERMANY ANNOUNCED that it was ending its agreement to stop attacking civilian ships. Six weeks later, three American merchant ships were sunk by German U-boats. In response, the United States declared war on Germany on April 6, 1917. The vast majority of the American people were in favor of going to war, but America's armed forces were small and ill-prepared. Volunteers were slow to enlist, and a national **draft** was established to enlarge the army.

A small force arrived in Paris on July 4, 1917. At a cemetery in the French captial, **General John J. Pershing** placed a wreath on the grave of the Marquis de Lafayette. Lafayette had come to America in 1777 to help fight in the American Revolution. In a speech, American colonel Charles E. Stanton declared "Lafayette, nous voilà," which in English means, "Lafayette, we are here." It was a promise to return France's support of American independence with American support in France's hour of need. Before the year was out, 180,000 American troops would be fighting in France.

Only a small number of Americans opposed the war and the draft. However, the government took measures to suppress them.

A British tank travels the streets of New York City during a 1917 parade.

"*It is . . . always like this in a field hospital. Just ambulances rolling in, and dirty, dying men.***"**

—AMERICAN NURSE
ELLEN LA MOTTE, 1934

CHAPTER 20

WOMEN IN WAR

Women played important roles
on both sides in the war.

THE WAR WAS NOT FOUGHT ENTIRELY by men. Military nurses cared for the wounded and dying in hospitals, but they were often in short supply. As a result, many civilian women volunteered to do this important work. One of the first American nurses to serve in Europe in the early days of the war was Ellen La Motte. She later wrote a book about her experiences in a French field hospital. The book was so graphic in its depiction of the horrors of war that it was suppressed and not republished until 1934.

Many other women in the United States, Great Britain, Germany, and Russia took over the jobs of men who had left for the war. They worked in factories, drove buses, and filled many other important roles.

In 1917, the U.S. Navy enlisted women to serve in non-nursing support roles for the first time. These women performed jobs such as operating radio equipment, delivering messages, and taking notes during meetings.

Male and female workers inspect bomb shells at a British munitions factory in 1917.

*Machine guns allowed soldiers
to fire bullets at their enemies
very quickly. That didn't stop
Sergeant York.*

CHAPTER 21

SERGEANT YORK, AMERICAN HERO

The war's most famous heroes inspired fellow
soldiers to keep fighting during tough times.

AMONG THE AMERICAN HEROES OF World War I, few were more celebrated than <u>Alvin York</u>. Raised in a poor family in the hills of Tennessee, he was an expert marksman. York was drafted and sent to France.

On October 8, 1918, he was on a mission with other American soldiers in the Argonne Forest. They were spotted and fired on by a unit of German machine gunners. Nine American soldiers were killed or wounded. York started firing back. When the shooting was over, he had killed more than 20 of the enemy. His example inspired his remaining comrades, and they also begain firing. The German commander believed they were being attacked by a large group and surrendered. York and his handful of companions marched the 132 German prisoners 10 miles (16 km) to the American headquarters.

York's life was captured in a popular 1941 movie, Sergeant York, which starred Gary Cooper in the title role.

Alvin York was the most decorated American soldier of World War I.

Posters like this one featuring the character Uncle Sam encouraged Americans to join the military and help win the war.

CHAPTER 22

PROPAGANDA: THE WAR OF WORDS AND IMAGES

Influencing people's opinions about the enemy

was an important part of the war effort.

PROPAGANDA PLAYED A CRUCIAL ROLE IN the war. Colorful war posters inspired patriotism and persuaded men to enlist in the armed services and fight. German propaganda claimed that an Allied victory would mean "the end of the German people." On the other hand, in one graphic American poster, Germany is depicted as a savage ape carrying a club in one hand and a captured woman in the other. The text reads "Destroy this mad brute. Enlist."

Anti-German propaganda had a dark side, helping fuel intolerance among Americans of anything German. Many German Americans were verbally and even physically abused by their neighbors. German books were removed from libraries, and many American orchestras stopped performing the music of German composers such as Beethoven.

Check it out!

A U.S. armed forces recruitment poster from 1917

*Black soldiers pose for a photo
on the trip home from Europe
after the war.*

CHAPTER 23

AFRICAN AMERICAN SOLDIERS

Racism followed black soldiers into the war, but it didn't stop them from serving their country.

AFRICAN AMERICANS WERE DRAFTED IN higher numbers proportionally than white Americans during World War I. The vast majority of black recruits were put in **segregated**, noncombat positions—delivering supplies, doing menial labor, or serving as cooks—because many Americans held racist beliefs. Some did not want to give black people guns for fear they would incite violence on American soil. Others believed that black soldiers weren't capable of fighting bravely. But attitudes began to change toward the end of the war as more soldiers were needed.

Most black soldiers were segregated into the 92nd and 93rd Divisions. One all-black **regiment** of New York volunteers, the 369th Infantry, was sent to France in 1918. Its members fought bravely and were nicknamed the Harlem Hellfighters. The Hellfighters received the French Croix de Guerre, a medal awarded to soldiers from Allied countries for bravery in combat. They later became the first American soldiers to reach the Rhine River in Germany. Their exploits changed many Americans' attitudes toward black soldiers.

A black soldier laughs during a gas mask drill.

*Traditionally, armies marched
into battle to the beat of a drum.*

CHAPTER 24

SONGS OF WAR

American soldiers had marched into battle
to music since the American Revolution, and
they carried on this tradition in World War I.

BEFORE THE UNITED STATES ENTERED THE war, antiwar songs like "I Didn't Raise My Boy to Be a Soldier" reflected the feelings of many Americans. But as attitudes changed, so did the music. Soldiers went off to France singing "Good-bye Broadway, Hello France." People back home heard the comedic "How Ya Gonna Keep 'Em Down on the Farm After They've Seen Paree? (Paris)" and wondered if soldiers would want to come back to America after seeing the wonders of Europe.

The most popular war song of all was "Over There" by Broadway songwriter George M. Cohan. At a time when recorded music was still uncommon, "Over There" sold two million copies of sheet music. Cohan donated all his proceeds from the song to war charities. This act of generosity earned him the Congressional Medal of Honor.

Sheet music is a set of printed instructions for playing a song on a musical instrument.

Allied troops participate in a sing-along during their downtime in 1916.

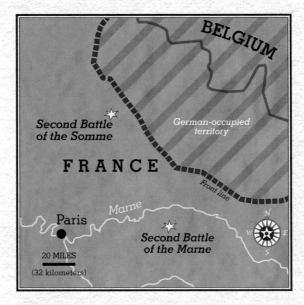

BELGIUM

Second Battle
of the Somme

German-occupied
territory

FRANCE

Front line

Marne

Paris

Second Battle
of the Marne

N
W   E
S

20 MILES
(32 kilometers)

CHAPTER 25

THE WAR REACHES A CROSSROADS

American forces in Europe helped
turn the tide of the war in 1918.

BY THE START OF 1918, BOTH SOLDIERS AND civilians alike were exhausted and ready for combat to end. The Central powers, however, were worse off than the Allies. On March 21, 1918, the Germans launched their last major offensive. Once again, the Somme River was the scene of a massive battle. In the Second Battle of the Somme, Germans drove British troops back several miles, making the single largest gain of the war since 1914.

By May, the Germans had pushed through to the Marne River, just 40 miles (64 km) from Paris. American troops, most of them inexperienced in combat, were called in as reinforcements. They surprised the Germans and drove them back across the Marne. On July 15, the Germans attacked again. The Second Battle of the Marne, as this battle was known, took a heavy toll on the once-invincible German army. Soon they were in full retreat.

French soldiers stand among the ruins of a cathedral during the Second Battle of the Marne.

*A woman in Ohio reads
headlines announcing the
end of the war in 1918.*

CHAPTER 26

THE WAR'S END

One by one, the Central powers fell like
a house of cards. Germany now stood alone.

TIME WAS RUNNING OUT FOR THE CENTRAL powers. Bulgaria surrendered on September 30, 1918. Turkey signed a peace treaty on October 30, after Allied forces captured major cities in Syria and Lebanon. Austria-Hungary gave up on November 3, after being weakened by uprisings by ethnic Czechs, Hungarians, and Yugoslavs.

On its own, Germany's iron discipline finally broke. German defeats had made the kaiser unpopular with the country's people. Mobs rioted against him in Berlin and other cities. A mutiny erupted in the navy. In Munich, a communist revolution flared. The kaiser, fearing for his life, **abdicated** on November 9 and fled to the Netherlands. Germany was declared a **republic**, with a **socialist** as president.

On November 11, 1918, representatives of the new German government met with Allied leaders in France and signed an **armistice**. The war was over. People in Allied countries rejoiced as their soldiers returned. The German people were bitter and angry. They had been sure all along that their country would win the war.

Crowds celebrate the armistice in November 1918.

JUNE 28

The six-month-long Paris Peace Conference ends with Germany and the Allies signing the Treaty of Versailles.

1919 JAN FEB MAR APR MAY JUN JUL

CHAPTER 27

THE TREATY OF VERSAILLES

The peace treaty changed the face of Europe
and broke the spirit of the defeated Germans.

IN JANUARY 1919, THE ALLIES HELD A conference in Paris to arrange the terms for peace. The six-month peace conference was dominated by the "Big Four"—American president Woodrow Wilson, British **prime minister David Lloyd George**, French **premier Georges Clemenceau**, and Italian prime minister Vittorio Emanuele Orlando. Germany, much to its frustration, had no say in the conditions of peace.

The map of the world was changed. The new nations of Czechoslovakia (now the Czech Republic and Slovakia) and Yugoslavia (now seven independent nations, including Serbia and Croatia) were formed. Poland was rebuilt as a nation. Four countries of the now defunct Russian Empire—Finland, Estonia, Latvia, and Lithuania—gained independence.

Little mercy was shown to the defeated Germans. Their armed forces were shrunk to nearly nothing, and they were saddled with an undetermined amount of **reparations** to be paid to the Allies. The Treaty of Versailles was finally signed on June 28. Separate treaties were signed later with the other defeated Central powers.

World leaders gather to sign the Treaty of Versailles in France in 1919.

Versailles is the elaborate palace of French kings built by Louis XIV outside Paris in 1682.

" *For several days there were no coffins and the bodies piled up something fierce. . . . It beats any sight they ever had in France after a battle.* **"**

—LETTER WRITTEN ON SEPTEMBER 29, 1918,
BY A DOCTOR AT CAMP DEVENS,
A MILITARY BASE NEAR BOSTON

CHAPTER 28

THE GREAT PANDEMIC

The war was over, but death
continued to stalk the world.

AN INFLUENZA **PANDEMIC** SWEPT through Europe starting in 1918. It was inaccurately nicknamed the Spanish flu. (Spain, one of the few neutral European nations during the war, gave widespread coverage to the flu's progress, while other nations censored the grim news as the war continued.)

The flu had originated with a few cases in Kansas. U.S. servicemen brought the flu with them to Europe where it mutated, or changed, becoming deadlier. Many soldiers who had survived the war died of the flu. When U.S. soldiers returned home, the virus came back with them. It quickly spread to 46 states, and by December 1918 it had caused more than 500,000 deaths in the United States.

Sick people were **quarantined** in their homes to prevent the spread of the flu. Schools, theaters, and churches closed to prevent people from gathering and spreading germs. Before the pandemic was over at the end of 1919, the influenza took 20 million to 50 million lives worldwide, far more than the 17 million who had died in the war. It remains the deadliest pandemic in history.

Unlike other viruses, this form of the flu was most deadly to young adults.

An influenza patient lies in bed at a U.S. Army hospital in New York in 1918.

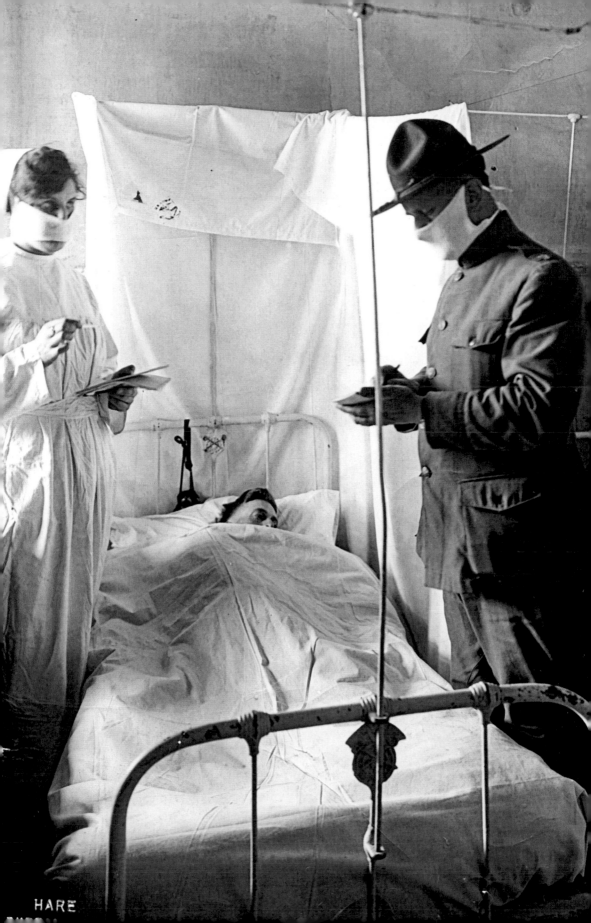
HARE

The League of Nations' official logo

CHAPTER 29

THE LEAGUE OF NATIONS

The League of Nations was formed to prevent
future wars, but it was doomed from the start.

THE TREATY OF VERSAILLES ESTABLISHED an international organization that would help peacefully resolve differences between countries. It was called the League of Nations. President Wilson had long dreamed of such an organization. But Americans were in no mood to join it. After the war, a wave of **isolationism** swept the country. Many felt that the United States could be safe only if it avoided involvement with foreign countries.

Wilson crisscrossed the nation in 1919 in an effort to gather support for the League of Nations. But on March 19, 1920, the U.S. Senate voted against joining it. Without the United States, the League of Nations would not succeed. It failed to act against the aggressive acts of rising dictatorships in Germany and Italy in the 1930s, leading to World War II.

The League of Nations disbanded in 1946, the year after a new and more effective international organization, the United Nations, was established. This time, the United States played a major role in the new organization's founding.

The commissioners of the League of Nations gather for a photo in 1920.

SOCIÉTÉ des NATIONS

ENTRÉE des DÉLÉGUÉS

66 *We have won the war. Now we will have to win the peace. That may prove harder.* 99

—FRENCH PREMIER GEORGES CLEMENCEAU ON NOVEMBER 11, 1918, THE DAY OF THE ARMISTICE

CHAPTER 30

A WORLD IN TATTERS

The war was over, but its legacy lived on.

THE COST OF WORLD WAR I WAS EXTREMELY high. About 10 million military personnel died, including more than 2 million Germans, 1.4 million French, and 117,000 Americans. The total number of civilians killed is estimated to be 13 million. Both the victors and the vanquished were left exhausted and impoverished. In most European countries, there was a shortage of able-bodied men to run businesses. Survivors were weakened by food shortages. France and Great Britain owed tremendous war debts. Germany, already close to economic collapse, was burdened with war reparations that it could not pay.

Desperate to find a better future, Germany turned to a new leader named Adolf Hitler, who would outdo Kaiser Wilhelm in his thirst for power. After just 20 years of peace, a new and even more terrible world war would darken all of Europe.

People gather to remember fallen soldiers at a British graveyard in 1919.

Kaiser Wilhelm II of Germany wanted more power and territory for his country and urged Austria-Hungary to declare war on Serbia. Once it did, Germany followed.

President Woodrow Wilson (1913–21) of the United States did not want to go to war and kept America out of the fray until German aggression against American merchant ships left him little choice. Once in the war, he proved a strong leader.

Prime Minister David Lloyd George of Great Britain was at first opposed to war but became a strong war leader as his country battled Germany. He played an active role in the creation of the Treaty of Versailles at the war's end.

Premier Georges Clemenceau of France was known as the Tiger of France. He presided over the Paris conference and demanded severe terms for Germany.

Czar Nicholas II of Russia was quick to come to the aid of Serbia. However, the war became unpopular in Russia and led to a revolution that removed Nicholas from power and ended Russia's participation in the war.

Winston Churchill, Great Britain's first lord of the Admiralty, planned a land attack at Gallipoli in Turkey that was meant to reopen the water route to Russia. The plan failed miserably, and Churchill was forced to resign.

General John J. Pershing, commander of the American Expeditionary Forces in Europe, shaped his troops into a powerful fighting force. After the war, he was named general of the armies of the United States, the highest rank ever given to a U.S. army officer.

Manfred von Richthofen of Germany, known as the Red Baron, was the greatest flying ace of World War I. He shot down 80 Allied airplanes before he was killed.

WORLD WAR I TIMELINE

JUNE 28

*Archduke Franz
Ferdinand of Austria-
Hungary and his wife
are assassinated.*

OCTOBER 29

*The Ottoman Empire
joins the Central
powers of Germany and
Austria-Hungary.*

DECEMBER 24

The Christmas Truce

1914 JAN FEB MAR APR MAY **JUN** JUL AUG **SEP** **OCT** NOV **DEC** **1915** JAN FEB MAR

JULY 28

*The war begins: Austria-
Hungary declares war on
Serbia. Germany supports
Austria-Hungary. France,
Russia, and Great Britain
join Serbia's side.*

SEPTEMBER 6–9

*In the Battle of the Marne,
the French beat back the
Germans from Paris.*

APRIL 25
Allied troops land on Turkey's Gallipoli Peninsula, only to retreat after devastating losses by the year's end.

MAY 7
A German submarine sinks the British passenger ship Lusitania, *killing nearly 1,200 people.*

MAY 31
The Battle of Jutland is fought by British and German warships off the coast of Denmark.

APR MAY JUN JUL AUG SEP OCT NOV DEC **1916** JAN **FEB** MAR APR **MAY** JUN **JUL** AUG SEP

APRIL 22
Germany uses poison gas as a weapon for the first time at the Second Battle of Ypres in Belgium.

FEBRUARY 21
The Battle of Verdun begins as Germans assault the French fortress town.

JULY 1
The Battle of the Somme begins in northern France and lasts more than five months.

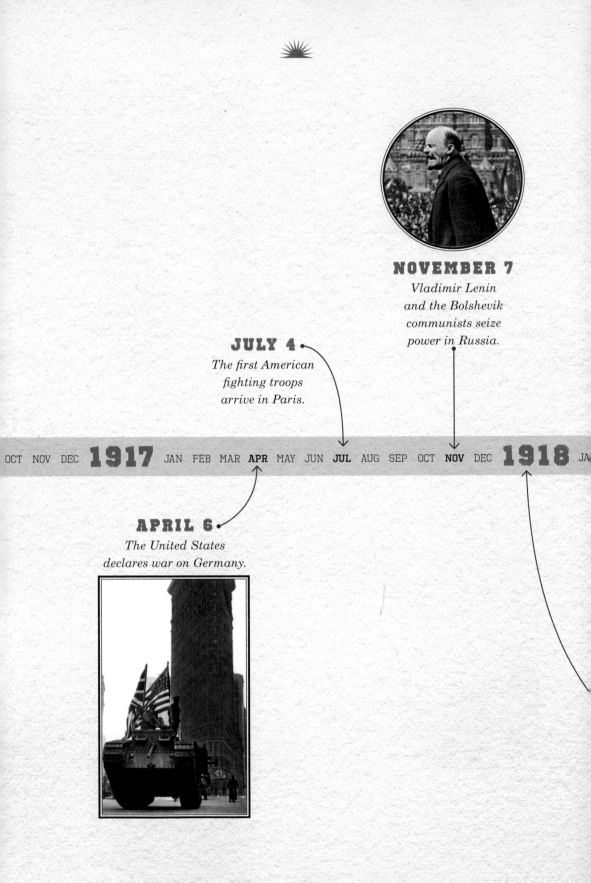

NOVEMBER 7
*Vladimir Lenin
and the Bolshevik
communists seize
power in Russia.*

JULY 4
*The first American
fighting troops
arrive in Paris.*

OCT NOV DEC **1917** JAN FEB MAR **APR** MAY JUN **JUL** AUG SEP OCT **NOV** DEC **1918** JA

APRIL 6
*The United States
declares war on Germany.*

NOVEMBER 3
*Austria-Hungary
surrenders to
the Allies.*

JUNE 28
*The six-month-long Paris Peace
Conference ends with Germany
and the Allies signing the
Treaty of Versailles.*

OCTOBER 8
*Private Alvin York and a
small group of American
soldiers kill more than
30 Germans and capture
another 132.*

FEB MAR APR MAY JUN JUL AUG SEP **OCT** **NOV** DEC **1919** ... JUN ... **1920** JAN FEB

NOVEMBER 11
*The Germans sign
the armistice, ending
World War I.*

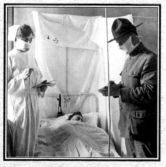

JANUARY 19
*The League of Nations
is formed to promote
peace between nations,
but the United States
does not join.*

1918–19
*The great influenza
pandemic begins. By the
end of 1919, it will have
taken 20 million to 50
million lives worldwide.*

GLOSSARY

- **abdicated** (AB-di-kate-id) gave up power

- **alliances** (uh-LYE-uhns-iz) agreements to work together for some result

- **armistice** (AHR-mus-tus) a temporary agreement to stop a war

- **artillery** (ahr-TIL-ur-ee) large, powerful guns that are mounted on wheels or tracks

- **Bolshevik** (BOHL-shuh-vik) a member of a radical political party that advocated the seizing of power in Russia by the workers and common people

- **bunkers** (BUHNG-kurz) underground shelters

- **casualties** (KA-zhul-teez) people who are injured or killed in an accident, a natural disaster, or a war

- **draft** (DRAFT) a system that requires people to serve in the armed forces

- **front** (FRUHNT) the area where two armies meet and fight

- **infantry** (IN-fuhn-tree) the foot soldiers of an army

- **isolationism** (eye-suh-LAY-shuhn-izm) the policy of keeping a country from participating in foreign affairs

- **neutral** (NOO-truhl) not supporting or agreeing with either side of a disagreement or competition

- **pandemic** (pan-DEM-ik) an outbreak of disease that affects a very large region or the whole world

- **peninsula** (puh-NIN-suh-luh) a piece of land that sticks out from a larger landmass and is almost completely surrounded by water

- **propaganda** (prah-puh-GAN-duh) information that is spread to influence the way people think, to gain supporters, or to damage an opposing group

- **province** (PRAH-vins) a district or region of some countries

- **quarantined** (KWOR-uhn-teend) kept away from others for a period of time to stop a disease from spreading

- **regiment** (REJ-uh-muhnt) a military unit of ground forces

- **reparations** (reh-puh-RAY-shuhnz) money paid by a defeated nation to the victors for damages or losses in war

- **republic** (rih-PUHB-lik) a form of government in which the people have the power to elect representatives who manage the government; republics often have presidents

- **segregated** (SEG-rih-gate-id) kept apart in separate groups

- **socialist** (SOH-shuh-list) a person who supports an economic system in which the government, rather than private individuals, owns and operates the factories, businesses, and farms

FIND OUT MORE

BOOKS

Adams, Simon. *World War I*. New York: DK Educational Books, 2007.

Atwood, Kathryn J. *Women Heroes of World War I*. Chicago: Chicago Review Press, 2016.

Hallihan, Kerrie Logan. *In the Fields and the Trenches: The Famous and the Forgotten on the Battlefields of World War I*. Chicago: Chicago Review Press, 2016.

Hasek, Jaroslav. *The Good Soldier Svejk*. New York: Penguin, 2005 [reprint].

Hemingway, Ernest. *A Farewell to Arm*s. New York: Scribner, 2014 [reprint].

Remarque, Erich Maria. *All Quiet on the Western Front*. New York: Ballantine Books, 1987 [reprint].

FILMS

All Quiet on the Western Front (1930). DVD, Universal Studios Home Entertainment, 2007.

Gallipoli (1981). DVD, Paramount, 2013.

Paths of Glory (1957). DVD, MGM, 2006.

Shoulder Arms (1918). In The Essential Chaplin, DVD, Cobra Entertainment, 2010.

NOTE: Some books and films may not be appropriate for younger viewers.

VISIT THIS SCHOLASTIC WEB SITE FOR
MORE INFORMATION ABOUT **WORLD WAR I**
www.factsfornow.scholastic.com
Enter the keywords **WORLD WAR I**

INDEX

Page numbers in *italics* indicate illustrations.

African Americans, *102*, 104, *105*

air battles, *66*, 68, *69*, 135

Allied powers, 12, *12*, 28, 29, 32, 52, 112, 116, 120

armistice, *114*, 116, *117*, 130, 139

artillery, *22*, 36, 60

Austria-Hungary, 12, *12*, 16, 24, 28, 116, 134, 136, 139

Battle of Jutland, *62*, 64, *65*, 137

Battle of the Marne, *34*, 36, *37*, 136, *136*

Battle of the Somme, 76, 137

Battle of Verdun, *70*, 72, *73*, 76, 137

Belgium, *26*, 28, 60, 137

Brooke, Rupert, 42, 44

Bulgaria, 116

Canada, 68

casualties, 24, 44, 52, 56, 60, 64, 68, 84, 96, 124, 132, *133*

Central powers, 12, *12*, 28, 29, 32, 52, 112, 116, 120, 136

chemical weapons, *58*, 60, *61*, 137, *137*

Christmas Truce, *46*, 48, *49*

Churchill, Winston, 52, 135, *135*

Clemenceau, Georges, 120, 130, 134, *134*

communists, *82*, 84, 116, 138, *138*

Czechoslovakia, 120

eastern front, 40, *49*

equipment, *14*, *18*, 36, *38*, 60, *61*

France, 12, *12*, 16, *17*, 24, 28, *34*, 36, *37*, 40, 44, 52, 60, *66*, 72, *73*, 76, 80, 88, 96, 104, 112, *113*, 116, 120, *121*, 130, 132, 134, 136, 137

Franco-Prussian War, 16, *17*

Franz Ferdinand, archduke of Austria-Hungary, *22*, 24, *25*, 136, *136*

Gallipoli, *50*, 52, *53*, 135, 137

Germany, 12, *12*, 16, *17*, *18*, 20, 28, 36, 40, *41*, *45*, 46, 48, *49*, *54*, 56, 60, *61*, 64, *65*, 68, 72, 76, 80, 84, 88, 92, 96, 100, 104, 112, 116, 120, 128, 132, 134, 136, 137, 138, 139

Great Britain, 12, *12*, 16, 20, *26*, 28, 42, 48, 52, *53*, 56, 64, 76, *77*, *89*, 92, 112, 120, 132, *133*, 134, 135, 136, 137

Hitler, Adolf, 132

influenza, 122, 124, *125*, 139, *139*

Italy, 16, 28, 128

Kennedy, John F., 44

La Motte, Ellen, 90, 92

League of Nations, *126*, 128, *129*, 139, *139*

Lenin, Vladimir, 82, *82*, 84, *85*, 138, *138*

Lloyd George, David, 120, 134, *134*

Lusitania passenger ship, 56, *57*, 137, *137*

machine guns, 36, 68, *94*, 96

maps, *12*, *13*, *34*, *50*, *62*, *70*, *86*, *110*

Marquis de Lafayette, 88

Mata Hari, 80, *81*

music, 100, *106*, 108, *109*

naval battles, 64, *65*, 137

Nicholas II, czar of Russia, 28, *29*, 84, 135, *135*

Ottoman (Turkish) Empire, 28, 52, 116, 136

pandemic, 122, 124, *125*, 139, *139*

Pershing, John J., 88, 135, *135*

poetry, 42, 44

Poland, 120

Princip, Gavrilo, 24, 136

propaganda, *98*, 100, *100*, *101*

Richthofen, Manfred von, 68, 135, *135*

Russia, 16, 28, 52, 82, *82*, 84, *85*, 92, 120, 135, 136, 138, *138*

Second Battle of the Marne, *110*, 112, *113*

Second Battle of Ypres, 60, 137

Serbia, 28, 120, 134, 135, 136

Sophie, duchess of Hohenberg, *22*, 24, *25*

Soviet Union, 84

spies, *78*, 80, *81*

Stanton, Charles E., 88

submarines, *54*, 56, 64, 88, 137

tanks, 74, 76, *77*, *89*

Treaty of Versailles, *118*, 120, *121*, 128, 134, 139, *139*

trenches, *38*, 40, *41*, 44, *45*

United States, 12, *30*, 32, 44, 56, 68, 80, 82, 88, *89*, 92, *98*, 100, *101*, 108, 112, 120, 124, *125*, 128, 132, 134, 135, 138, 139

weapons, 36, 56, *58*, 60, 72, 76, *93*, *94*, 137

western front, *13*, 40, 48, *86*

Wilhelm II, kaiser of Germany, 20, *21*, 116, 132, 134, *134*

Wilson, Woodrow, 32, *33*, 56, 120, 128, 134, *134*

women, 92, *93*

York, Alvin, 96, *97*, 139, *139*

ABOUT THE AUTHOR

Steven Otfinoski has written more than 180 books for young readers. They include books about the sinking of the *Lusitania*, heroic soldiers in World War I, and other books about wars involving the United States. Three of his books have been named to the New York Public Library's list of recommendations, Books for the Teen Age. He lives with his family in Connecticut.

Maps by Jim McMahon.